1st Edition

ADVANCE COPY
SEE LETTER

C0-AMA-274

811.5
Van

146540

Van Doren.
New poems.

Learning Resources Center
Nazareth College of Rochester, N. Y.

MARK VAN DOREN

WILLIAM SLOANE ASSOCIATES, INC.
Publishers *New York*

WITHDRAWN
LEARNING RESOURCES CENTER
NAZARETH COLLEGE

"A Hundred Minnows" (page 88), copyright 1945 by Mark Van Doren, "He's Coming" (page 67), and "Then Both Shall Be" (page 109), copyright 1946 by the F-R. Publishing Corporation (*The New Yorker*).

Copyright, 1948, by
Mark Van Doren

First printing

146540

Printed in the United States of America
Published simultaneously in Canada by George J. McLeod Ltd., Toronto

811.5
Van

Contents

WORDS FOR MUSIC MORE OR LESS

The author wishes to thank the following magazines for permission to reprint the poems which they first published: *Briarcliff Quarterly, Columbia Review, Harper's Magazine, Harvard Alumni Bulletin, Harvard Wake, Household, Kenyon Review, Ladies' Home Journal, Nation, Partisan Review, Poetry Quarterly* (*London*), *Saturday Evening Post, Saturday Review of Literature, Sewanee Review, Virginia Quarterly Review, Woman's Home Companion, Yale Review* copyright Yale University Press. "A Hundred Minnows," "He's Coming," and "Then Both Shall Be" originally appeared in the *New Yorker*. Some of the poems in this book were first printed in THE COUNTRY YEAR and THE CARELESS CLOCK.

THE SUN ONCE ROSE

The Sun Once Rose

The sun once rose from off a watery couch,
And soaring daylong, sank to cool again.
The eastern, western seas were limitless,
Worlds of deep dew, a double and old home
Dry light was not a friend to. But he climbed,
He curved, and he descended. So our fathers
Fabled him, gold ornament of skies.

But now he never sleeps. No dark, no wet
Receives him. Hot and high, he burns his way
Forever round the world, whose distant oceans
Parch him. He himself is cause of noon,
Monotonous. The ball he sees below
Turns the same satin side with every solstice.
Daylong is what he lives in; and would die.

Yet not for him the sweetness of such dusks
As rose an hour to meet his father, falling.
Delicate that death: a labor's end,
As dawn was end before it. Then day lived
As men do, twixt eternities so soft
That womb and grave are blessings. Or would be
If so they lived as once the sun did, soaring.

When Will True Love Again

When will true love again make delicate difference
In the deep place where old foundations dream;
Where stone on stone they lie; yet they can slip,
Can settle, even in sleep: earthquake adjustment,
Answering our joy. When, single again,
Will a good heart cause all the world to shiver?

Or evil; for the children of men tell
How once the stain spread on and on: to stars
That darkened, and down, down to the same old stones,
That shuddered, their vast surfaces set grinding
And groaning as the universe endured
The peril of one face that hid the fiend.

There was a time, grandchildren of God say,
When one soul made the difference; when each life
Was more, was less, was counted. This machine
Above us dropped no shadow on them then.
It was not here, and high; it was not more
Than men were. It is ours alone, this giant,

This gear within smooth gear, this mounting spiral
Rooted in no rock, but spinning there
Topheavy with late time. Cause over cause
It rises, and fills all the sky with wheels,
With history that clangs upon the ear,
The small ear of the listener, the lone one.

When he was single, and the sun burned on him,
He was no lone one; then he was companioned
By the sheer weight he bore, by very worlds
That waited till he should be foul or clean.
Now he but creeps, a something with pale wings,
A colorless poor cricket, listening.

He has his labors still, and his fine loves.
He comes on others, tiny in this shade,
And muzzles them. Antenna to antenna,
It is a tender meeting. But no more
Do the stones know, the faraway great fissures
That once decision's thunder shook and filled.

The Stranger's Tale

Two ages pursue each other under the sun.
Either outlasts memory; no chronicle
Tells of their alternation. Yet old songs
Sing of the wondrous difference when gods
Gather again; when men, lone in the wind,
Are suddenly revisited, and guardians
Temper all effort, sowing the earth with ease.

Then apples are eternal; beasts are friends,
And drink from the same never icy waters.
Then do no hearts dispute; each eye is ample,
Owning as much of azure as it sees,
As much of soil, of thicket. Where grapes hang
And melons lie, where generous birds give music,
There every foot both wanders and keeps home.

In the gold age gods are as close together
As the ripe plums that cluster; are as close
To movers in the meadow as moths come,
Kissing the daisy white. But they are huge,
These fathers, and keep faith with their soft children,
Those souls with no tomorrow, those unmeaning
Foster folk that play at being men.

Or so men say when deity, departed,
Leaves them to dig and harrow; brings the frost;
And huddles certain of them in wild cities,

Woeful yet necessary, whose hard laws
Build peace instead of music. For the tune
That sang itself is lost, and torturers
Wring harmony from rock, from gravel's word.

This is the time of man, the terrible,
The artful time, the beautiful with risk.
And none then will exchange it, though pure songs
Sing of the wondrous difference. No man then
Would save himself more easily. The time
Is his alone, to dignify or mar;
His only gold is rule, is government.

But the first age is waiting, or the last,
When men again shall be as sparrows are,
With providence for watcher, and no skill
To ruin what is round them, or to scheme
Amends. There is no peril on the path
For deity's dark foundlings. Whom we sing,
Remembering, then with sharpened gaze forget.

The Case Is New

Good monarchs have been monarchs of themselves;
The ruler was a thing that could be ruled.
But rare the case, and now that princes perish,
How will the many govern save by good?
And how then will they look both out and in,
Command and be commanded? For the case
Is new, it still is new, and no man standing
Misses in wind rumors of sour success.

For the good king was stranger, and his crown,
A sunborn jewel, dazzled the clearest eyes.
He was a soul descended, and men rose
To meet him. So they swore. That time is gone,
With all of its grim witnesses. Another
Comes; the many now must learn to rise
And overflow themselves. Yet what the yeast,
And whence, and how to keep it sweet within?

For centuries, forever, it must live,
The sweet germ within; and each must bear it,
A small seed in his heart; each be a king
Commanded, and each able to command.
There never was such task, there never trembled
Such a huge world of trouble being born.
For each separate cell must keep its smallness,
In a good heart that nothing overgrows.

The multitude is lesser than its members.
But it can swell to monster if the seeds
Within it be not sound and know their size.
Let each enlarge with the good king for limit,
The ruler and the ruled. Then the huge whole
Is leavened, and long happiness appears—
Oh, when? And by what magic will all men
Discover friend and stranger in one room?

The Long Life and the Short Life

The long life and the short life differ dimly
In the midwood where even noon is dark.
Do those about to die see both, and clearly,
Through the late hour when weakness is at work?
In the far field of sunset do they show
Like two unequal mountains, tall and low?

Too late to choose then? Is it middle still,
The wide road of that wandering? Does space
Slumber as now? Is time, the dreary ocean,
Tempestless yet: eternity awash?
Then I shall look about me in the wood,
Even by dusk, as if distinction stood.

And here it does if anywhere, I know:
Now, in the aisles of famous afternoon.
There have been thoughts that found it, under thickest
Mosses; there have been heroic men.
They led them both, the short life and the long.
Mere woodsmen, yet their wit was double strong.

They never shut their eyes against the shade.
They loved it well; and loved the outer light.
It shone in them all morning as they moved;
Unmentioned, for they would not walk apart.
Unsung, but it was what the others heard
Whenever, in still gloom, distinction stirred.

The little and the great life lie together
In a warm place eternity protects:
Midwood, among more branches than are dying.
For some of them cannot. This doom that cracks
Is timely; it is not for those that see
More difference than death, and doubly be.

SLOW LEARNING

Slow Learning

Intelligence all day upon us,
And every day, like snow in dark,
Inaudible, arrives unseen,
Impalpable; yet leaves its mark.

Or does it? O you dreamless skies
That flake upon us, do we change?
That shake upon us, do we show
As anything but dim and strange?

Still looking downward, as you do,
But from no zenith which were cause,
Are we so ignorant of white?
Do we break all of mirror's laws?

One face that turns, and taking you
Full on its water, on its glass:
Is it enough? And can you wait
For other centuries to pass

Till ten are there, till thousands shine,
Till all the lower world is love?
It has been long already, Light.
Or does it seem so, Sir, above?

The Sun So Old

The sun so old, the day so short—
What is it gives the heart a start
As stumbling I look up and see
This dome that was not made for me?

Why not before, when just as much
My life was poor, time's life was rich?
Why is it even truth must trim
This moment of my knowing him?

For there he sits, immense at last,
And disappears into the east;
And overstares the stiffened bow
Of one too late at learning how.

Little Places

Such power in little places:
The petal weight a coil of jelly moves,
And snails have conquered beaches.
The worm, with neither horn nor bone,
Plows acres.

Prometheus down a cold crack:
Rainstreams freezing, and the granite
Splits; as smoke of sister water
Pushes the long piston; and a copper
Hair holds worlds.

The Yes all year awaited:
Thinnest word, and yet it peoples spring
With mighty houses, lived in; No,
Enormous night; as when the bud bursts
Or does not.

Such power; with plants depending,
Thunder, and small men, and now the spark
Whereby a town is merry.
The end, that neither feels nor sees,
Thanks nothing.

When the New Growth No More Is Green

When the new growth no more is green,
And every summer's foliage fails,
The horny stem, the original,
Stands boastfully for all its ills.

When the sweet edges of doubt go,
Those gentle borders shy to the word,
How arrogantly spirit speaks;
How happy that the sound is hard.

But at the center even then
The dozy wood prepares to die;
And something honeycombs the bones
Of him that swears green truth away,

The curled, the tentative, that lives
Amid extremities of leaf,
And is more firm in any wind
Than he, original and stiff.

Death Indeed

So close death flew that when I walked away,
Still trembling, still stopped about the heart,
I walked as two men, and the livelier
Was he that had been stopped for good—yet came on
Standing, and revisits now all places
With someone lesser, with myself, the seen one.
Nobody notices. Which makes me wonder,
Had the wingbeat been final, whether death,
And death indeed, is not the walking on,
Just this way, of the selfsame legs and shoulders
And the fool's face of yesterday; yet lighted,
And with each weakness gone. For him I see
Is perfect in decision; him I hide
Is errorless, is angel. And I ponder,
After so many deaths, how full the world
Must be of his companions; for till then,
That day, I heard no rustle; and now even
Nothing I do reveals him, nothing I watch
And wince and cannot copy. It is death
Indeed that will unfasten him, my friend
Whom no one else can see; and someday no one.

Question

Do certainties, like persons being doubted,
Suffer? Solid persons, by their lovers
Doubted? There is difference: substantial
Flesh, that can survive the darkening in;
The core is gone, but color still in streaks
Says outwardly that something, someone is.
Are certainties so dogged against death,
Even unwillingly? Oh, did they ever
Hang there, did they ever in their turn
Be anyway, and only with our love
Be happy? Then be mocked with a bright form
That wore no visible wound accusing faith?
Do certainties, like persons, have both soul
And body? Or someday is our oblivion
Enemy to all? A sudden sun
That shrivels what was nothing but thought shade?
Not even nerved, like night? Not even mold?
Do certainties, like lovers being doubted,
Suffer? Solid lovers, that die twice?

Forever

Forever sings with a low sound
And level, swings a flat scythe, no felt thickness
Mocking men's shoes that must believe the sod.
Forever is a faith without dimension.
No foot finds it. Nor do noblest heads
Say it is their ceiling. For it skims
As innocent of place as the wind's pleasure;
Sings with a high sound too, that would be giddy
Music were it minded. Twixt two layers
Live we, high and low, of blade, of bird,
That even are the same: the wing is mower;
Weightlessly a sickle slices blue.
Forever sings to no end that is ours;
We breathe and die regardless, are not caused
As it is, nor escape into it after.
Forever sings forever, and the ears
That listen never have been here between.

Dirge

Time, with its terrible old hunger,
Devours our bodies one by one.
Still it is famished; looks for more;
And finding it, feeds on and on.

Whole pastures perish, the green custom withers
That nourished our once feeling souls.
Change cannot die, but change forgets;
Landscape can lose all its hills.

Our fathers buried more than flesh
When they lay down in their tall tombs.
So we grow sleepy with the slow
Death of bright meaning in these rooms.

Tools tarnish, and mansions settle,
Absurd, in swamps that pride had paved.
Justice sits on, but where they stood,
Those orators, salt water waves.

The private peace that all might have,
Or most, or some, where is it now?
The teeth have taken the last wall;
Moonlight is naked on your brow.

Statesman

Courage. If such a crowd,
More than you ever saw,
Seems wilderness—mankind's
Great plains of residue—

Remember as you go,
Taking yourself entire,
That two are there: the waste,
And he that would explore.

You also can be strange:
One man, and yet so much.
The goodness in you, whole,
Might garden them to speech.

That barrenness but seems.
One word has been enough,
Ere this, to plow and plant
And harvest it. Be off.

Let There Be Law

Wherever earth is home for men,
Beyond what mountains, by what seas,
Let honor and pride live; but now
Let there be law, transcending these.

Let there be law through all the world,
Whose children love their ancient lands.
May that love grow, but in the shade
Of justice's most mighty hands.

Let those be guardians of our strength,
Lest in long anarchy it cease.
May something deathless now be born.
Let law be father of our peace.

Song

Spring of the world again,
Oh, is there such a time:
Eternity of April,
Past hills, past green?

There will be grass again,
There will be buds, be lambs;
Here. But what of the outer
Spaces fate lives in?

Good of the heart again:
Can there be such a spring?
You everlasting winter,
Does it come on?

THE CLOSE CLAN

The Close Clan

Even from themselves they are a secret,
The like ones that dwell so far asunder:
So far, and yet the same; for gold is gold
In any earth, and thunder repeats thunder.

They are the scattered children of what pair,
What patient pair so long ago extinguished?
But the flesh lives, in certain ones that wind
And dust and simple being have distinguished.

Whatever these, and howsoever born,
They are the ones with perfect-lidded eyes,
Quieter than time, that yet can burn,
Can burn in rage and wonder and sunrise.

They are the ones that least of all the people
Know their own fewness, or the loving fear
Such lineage commands—that ancient couple,
And these their growth in grace's afteryear.

In them the world lives chiefly, as gold shines,
As thunder runs in mountains, and hearts beat.
They are the ones who comprehend the darkness,
And carry it all day, and sweeten it.

These Things

We could not love these things in others.
We should not love these things at all.
In him, though, they become themselves
As death does in vermilion fall.

We should not be so happy, seeing,
We should not feel so warm, under
The pinched green, and then the great,
The hectic bloom, disease's wonder.

We should not, yet the end of shade
Surpasses June; as he is more
God's likeness than a hundred good ones
Prismless at the clear core.

The rainbow of his hottest pride
Sits in red gold at the extremes.
Selfishness in him is painted
Soul. It flushes our white dreams.

Merriment in him, and anger—
Forgetful, then remembering us—
Are the autumnal teachers; are
Man in his blaze, miraculous.

The Black Woman

The big black woman smiled on this small earth
And on our eyes that thought the sun went down.
Down where? You cannot see it for the trees
And the thick air, she said, but it is bright
Forever, it is why our breasts are brown.

We face it all the way around the ring.
You only notice noonday and the dusk.
And one of these you call your looking glass,
And one you say is sleep. But that is when
We stir again with milk, and gather musk.

What you have named the night is when we stand,
Still nurses to the hours, and make them be.
They move in us; all time is but the scent
Of our soft patience. It is how I sit,
And how the merry world goes round with me.

And round. For it comes back to waken you,
And let you look as yesterday you did.
Up where, and whom do you see, and when the dark
comes,
What of your whiteness? It is not forever,
Ever, like the sun these breasts have hid.

Old Hundred

The blacksmith did not hobble here
To the small church, on the hard hill,
In summer, to be told of stars;
He came with meek and tempered will;
He came, this hoarest of bent men,
To hear Old Hundred sung again.

But the young voice above the Book
Praised Him who built the heaven's fires;
And the old listener grew still;
No congregations and no choirs
Were in the grave with him at last;
Nothing but him and the sweet vast,

Nothing but those he soon must lose
If death was losing; and death was.
He saw them, wonderful and old,
But with no power in them to pause
As they sailed on, as they sailed on,
Over his unmoving mound.

Little Servant

Little servant with the softer voice
Than hands among these hallways, be more loud
In laughing when the master sits at home.
With the same strength that makes the silver shine,
Shout in the dark rooms; be unafraid
Of coming and of going; tell quick tales
To windows, slam the doors, and on the stair,
Little servant, sing—sing in the proud way
Of wrens upon the ridges. For as much
You cause a house to be, as much you owe
The sky the pretty skill of your soft voice,
That only need be happier to fly here,
Fly there among the hallways—even to him,
The master in his gloom, who thinks he wants
All quiet, and queer shadows. But as much
As you and the shrill wrens he wishes heaven
For cover; and would have it if your song,
Little servant, lifted the whole roof.

Lady of Where She Lived

The round old lady with the little eyes—
Lady of where she lived, of the split shingle
Walls, and the warped door that let four cat feet,
Cat feet in—the white old one, she perished
Even as planned. For where she lived she was lady,
And the lamp knew it that she tilted over:
Tilted, and it poured obedient flame
Due upward till the cupboard papers caught.
There must have been more oil in secret places,
For the first valley warning was the last;
The windows were too bright, then not at all
In the one peak of red, the pyramid
She built, this queer old queen, to shrivel under.
The cat feet, cat feet fled among the highway
Asters, and they never felt again
For the gone door she must have heard them pressing
Till the warp freed them. They are wild now,
As she is, but they were not sacrificed.
She ended it alone. And lives alone
In the one place of which she could be lady,
The wild place of weeds; and of these clockworks,
Melted at the hour, the little minute,
He the lean one left her years ago.

When Rubies Were

They told this tale of her, that dying
She suffered robbers in the grave;
For ruby rings; that well were gone,
Since she awoke and time went on.

And time went on, and beauty bloomed
As if reborn in her twice bright;
For there was that about her gaze
Which glitters even to these days.

Even to these days come down,
Her beauty proves the story true;
As mystery is known to shine
In the found cask, the buried wine.

The buried wine our sun again
Sees into as the princes drink:
So must it once have been with her;
And so it was, when rubies were.

Bulletin

Did he seem happy? Well, he was serious;
Smiled, and was serious. But I saw
More than I used to in the difference,
More than I thought was possible there.

In him, in us, in anybody,
More than I thought could lie between
Quick kindness—you remember that—
And oh, so slow, the crooked shadow.

Yet it was difference I could measure.
He did not mix them. How he seemed?
Well, he is serious past saying.
And more of the old smile is smile.

Socratic

He suffered every fool alive,
But not as Lord and children.
He did not bless them, or predict
More light in them than could be.
They guttered, and he knew they would
Forever; yet he found them good.

We fled them, or we slept away
Long hours of them, of droning;
Of smoky wicks that were as smiles
Flattering confusion.
Familiar, but he liked it so;
And that was how he learned to know.

For he that stood, and shows the stain,
Is wiser still than we are.
The lamps we bear are brassy bright,
But he himself is lantern.
As they are. And if he is best,
He only claims him stubbornest.

Even than Water

He pushed him in and he held him down
Till no more struggle, and no more sound.

How many years had he hated that back
The crayfish fondled, and turtles perhaps?

Around it once met two white arms
With no more mercy in them than worms;

No more mercy upon him, standing—
Oh, right here; and again it was blinding,

Again it was dark, and he could not see
How too much silence soon would be;

How no more struggle, and no more sound
Would save her for him in dry ground;

Would give her to him, but quieter then
Even than water that sleeps with men.

The Five

The five terrible plutonian ogres
That ravaged separately five lands,
That ruled outrageously all folk,
Should have remained five. But once,
Remembering briskly they were brothers,
They left their mountains, and they met
And so were one again—their mother's
Marked brood, with similar hands,
With family eyes, and when they spoke,
One only voice, that memory sapped
Till each, an echo unto four,
Doubted his terror and was dunce.
The five returned, but not to ravage,
Not to rule. For the great glens,
Repeopled now and sodden savage,
Devoured them as a thing divided—
Five infants, huge and homeless,
Faint fifths of nothing any more.

The Fine Plan

The dust has long been settled that she rode,
A goddess in a buggy, with straight back
And blue ambitious gaze. For she was born
In a wild moment, and at twenty was taken
For better, worse, by husband and by pride.

And one of them is gone, but the other lives
As she does, thin in bed, remembering dust
And the hot horses; and when they were home,
The sons she would assess. For she could measure
By no rule but her own, that rode with her,

Superior to clouds; where now is clearness,
And weeds that have forgotten how she sped.
And strangers in that house. For we have scattered.
Only one gaunt lady will remember
What we were to have been, or what she was.

Here now she lies, with one of those she wedded
In the wild hour she fiercely lives again.
Here now she lies, and rages and refuses
All sixty years since that one; all poor time,
All persons, all that tempered the fine plan.

Odysseus

The broad-shouldered lord of rocky Ithaca,
Conqueror of brine, Athene's darling,
Listener to song and silent weeper
At his own name, Odysseus, loved himself
As the gods do, nor was it blasphemy.
The earth was in him, aching to be loved.

What man so happy, finding a sweet spring
Where nymphs hid and olive trees were old?
But it was blood to blood, as when his wrath
Sang swallow, and his bed postponed the dawn.
The pride of his own heart was strength's announcement;
Being in him boasted it was good.

The homecomer, shouting over waves
To the one world, his island, that it stand,
Even then was there; for all the globe
Rejoiced in him. Insulter of its giants,
Tamer of its sorcerers, he swam
Forgiven—greatness in him, and home ground.

Achilles

He that was deer was lion:
Fleet-footed, yet so huge
That Hector found him terrible
Nine years—and now,
Here where the fig tree stopped them,
Found no refuge.

He that was mother hearted—
Thetis, under the sea—
Robbed every mortal woman's
Tall son; and chilled,
Beside the bath that waited,
Andromache.

He that was wrath was pity,
Seeing another sire
In Priam when he trembled;
And his own doom
To be white bones in honey,
After hot fire.

HOMAGE TO SIX

To Homer

Master of ocean stream, those men you made
Were weaker than its waves, its bitter waves
With their deep smell of caverns never sounded.
Out of dry land you made them, out of dust,
Of bronze; and likened them to bees and lions,
And the lean cranes that flew. Smaller than gods,
Feebler than sun and thunder, less than hills
You reared them, and you set them far away,
Little in strength, from their dear native land.
Yet who so strong? For miracle is in them
Still; still their throats produce a music
Angry and long ago; their armor walks
As waves do, never resting; and their wills
Keep liberty no fate would comprehend.
Submissive to decree, they still are crowned,
Princes of themselves, and rule all verse
As one ruled then from Ida. What so strange,
Master of man's littleness, as this,
That still you most augment him? Still you give
Those governed ones the glory. Sovereign men
Through centuries since have been their subjects still;
And wondered at you too, lord of the sea waves.

Dante Alighieri

As if a cabinet became alive,
And the recesses in it, the small curios,
Burned with an equal being, the huge world
Let him come in; made itself little and patient;
Lasted in shape and singing till his eye,
His delicate ear, solved secrets and moved on.
He wound his way in miniature, beholding
All that can be in corners, all that can shine
In curves a candle, intense and sudden, shows.
But it went far and deep, that shelving place,
Till light itself, a penitent, broke sweetly
And swelled; and swelled again, beyond the mountain
Whose top was tawny spring; swelled, and in bursting
Circles blinded his thought. So he fell down
And down. Yet not to nowhere, for the cabinet
Kept him. As the brain holds every object,
Ticketed, in caverns, so this world
This man who most enlarged it; who with mouse steps
Measured its last echo, singing little,
Singing long of all that may be and that is.

To Chaucer

Those waves of understanding that arrived
Were the least ones. You let the long swells go
In their own darkness on around the world
Till they piled high and broke in afterwoe.

For you the choppy ones the sun had wrinkled.
They had come far too, and they still come on.
But in you then they rested. You gave forth
The sound they seek, of old men young at dawn;

Of men that have forgotten nothing woeful,
Yet at their waking smile. The world is fool
Forever, and its tears are not to cease.
But neither is this birdsong, high and cool,

This answer, like your own, to those least waves
That come with sunwarmth dappled on their crests:
The ones unseen except by old late men
And silly larks, up early in their nests.

To Shakespeare

Mankind had been so rank a field,
And you so knowing in its blossoms,
You were not lost, sir, but you came
Never home to other harvest.

Not lost, and yet no head appears,
No shoulders even, where you stood,
The tallest, surely, of those growths,
Overlooking them in wind.

Looking, moving, yet your feet
Have left no path. We cannot follow.
How many leagues to where you paused?
Was this the stile, sir, where you started?

You did not stumble back again
With your own sheaves to show and bind.
We shall not know you, sir, except
We go in after you and stand,

And overlook the waving souls
As once you did, in sun, in tempest,
Never turning or explaining,
Never singing of yourself, sir.

Thomas Hardy, Poet

With older eyes than any Roman had
In a stone hole, or Briton under barrow,
Steadily he gazed; and bleakest worlds
Grew warm—illicitly grew warm and moved;
For hope in him was backward, and love narrow.

Belief in him but squinted; God had died
Of palsy, and mankind, alone with feeling,
Was a poor skinless thing. Yet maids and squires,
Ghosts, organists, and gypsies, and small clerks
Mused in his tales, and oxen kept on kneeling.

It was a late hour and cold when he looked out:
The last man that remembered country singing.
And first to call it pitiful. Those folk
Outstayed themselves, he said. Yet as he listened,
Wanly, what sweet bell tongues took to swinging!

Emily Dickinson

Between her window and the maple tree
How many lines crisscrossed; yet none could see.

None but herself, for every object there
When she looked out was woven of tough air;

Was center to a web whose anchor pins
Were far as where Aldebaran begins.

Diameters of silk so intersected
That pit and pole and windowpane connected,

And a seen worm conducted her by rods
Of filament to Satan's house, to God's;

Where the fine nerve, inquiring, did not stay
For the long anthem, for the raven's lay.

The quicker bobolink meanwhile was home
And did as well the honors of this dome,

Immense and small, wherein her suffering plucked
String after string, that joy too could instruct.

TOO LONG AGO

146540

Too Long Ago

Those beautiful, young, breaking eyes:
Regard them and go on; they are not
Letting that forth which middle oldness
Ever again will understand.

One day when you are in the ground
They also will have hardened over:
Their beautiful young fear escaped,
Their fondness loose in the still world.

As yours is now, and let it be.
It cannot answer what they ask.
It is too everywhere and thin
For the new soul that seeks an image,

For the sweet beast that only now
Wakes out of it: the mother dark
Too long ago by you forgotten,
Too far away this latter evening.

LEARNING RESOURCES CENTER
NAZARETH COLLEGE

Proud Song

Let not the mover know,
Unmoved, the deep effect,
The spark that sometimes leaps,
The minnow in the flesh:
Sudden, the very self
Discovering to grow.

As if a father found,
One day, the infant plan
Cross charactered: a strange
Bird print upon an arm;
So let the first of all
In puzzlement be bound.

Whence are we? Let him search,
Unsure, in shaded time.
Let memory in him
Be startled by the mint,
Stepped on, of hidden mind
Outscenting the tall birch.

They Hurt Us Most

They hurt us most by loving us
And showing us they do.
Simplicity is sweetest then,
Yet harshest, tearing through.

The paper ring that might conceal
The pig, the tiger face—
When it is gone, and one of ours
Is there in his first grace,

The rent is here, not where the doubt
Across a circle stretched.
The sound is in the suddenness,
The pauperdom enriched.

Sullen Boy

Sullen boy, so knowing
And so downward—all is sloped,
Is tent ropes to the turf about your feet,
Is drooping slant away,
Is sadness home—

Sulky head, so loosely
Set there, stubborn threatener
To spill all countenance, to pour all courage
Groundward—have the grace,
For once, of fire,

Of lightest fire, that leaping,
And leaving, still companions us:
Though upward, yet remains, and with its eyes
Is faithful—be as that,
Downfalling boy.

You hunt the grass for cover,
The ravine where tulip shadows
Showed you once how sadness seeps away.
But burn it, and be still
Our vertical one.

The Soaked Ones

Where is that couple of slow boys,
Those downpour-lovers in drooped hats
Who on a day like this one went
And were to meadows as muskrats:

Disappearing in drowned hay
Before they shoved into a wood
That shook its great drops on their shoulders—
Overplus to what was good,

To what was falling everywhere
On those two lovers of wet death:
Of daring all that rain could do,
Entering, to put out breath?

For that was what their pride brought home,
Those dripping stampers up the stair;
Unwrapping the same spark they bore
Among arch-enemies of air.

Where is that brace of sober breasts,
Warm then before a second cause?
What dry logs now are laid for them
In what far land where Noah was?

The Ancient Couple on Lu Mountain

Into the pool of silence our tears made,
Our secret tears when lord son went away—
How straight his back among the willows was!—
Into this lake of time whereon our house
Is a small hidden island, nevertheless
Sound falls: a single dropping of sweet words,
With every moon, into this upland sea
That no crane visits, for the shores are lost.

Lord son is faithful. With each full of the moon
A letter comes here from the capital:
Comes dripping, dripping its clear characters
Like raindrops, one by one, into soft water.
No silence then. Yet afterward! yet now,
When the moon wanes; when memory grows weaker
Of the few musical, pure drops. How deep this pool is
Only the dark cranes know that never come.

Fecundity

Where now,
In swamp or mow,
In kitchen or in rank cheese room—
Where, in what sunny dream,
Do sixteen young ones at the loom, the plow,
The fire log, and the crock of cream,
Incontinent, come forth and swarm?

A dozen, four,
And then no more;
But that was plenty, that was hive.
Where, in what lone alcove,
Is honey builded now, is there uproar
Of legs and wings, of busy love,
Of singing lest the center starve?

Where at all
In this cold fall,
This season when wild growth is done?
Where, from what famished queen,
In some thin spring to come, will sixteen tall
Daughters and sons as from the lean
Loins of eternity be torn?

ONE THOUGHT OF IT

One Thought of It

One thought of it, the war, and horses
Trample a far fence, thundering off:
Thousands of wild goers, printing
Characters in alien sod.

One thought of it, the war, and manes there,
Flowing together, pile such a cloud
As smothers all boundary; and the thick neighing
Threatens, at home here, every sound.

One thought of it, the war, and herds
Climb the clear air, four-footed, clawing
At walls and stairways—all that was built there
Out of full chords, of custom's scales.

The Long War

The long war destroys
More than men and boys;
More than women sitting
Blastwise, knitting.
More than sill or frame
Where pretty morning came.

The long war is older
Than death is, and colder.
A slow thing; worse
Than moaning can rehearse;
So quietly it slays
Months, minutes, days.

So secretly it kills
Warmness in our wills;
Hope, and every end
To which time was friend.
The heart no longer bleeds
Whereon it creeps and feeds.

War's Distance

War's distance—how grotesque a fate
Distributes boys wherever trees are spread
Through difference's darkness; where I went
There were no lighted leaves.

Where he was the peninsula,
Palm feathered, put not forth a single name;
No needle smiled, declaring its known self;
The sun was a black lamp

Eclipsing even him, as pine,
As hemlock, as the oak, the ash, forgot
All north, and nothing shone between our eyes
Of the familiar shade.

We both were there, but not by day,
Though the sun's face was fierce, a Nubian wonder.
And love presided, but as death must do,
Superior to speaking.

Back to the War

Back to the war you go, down the long
Station steps, luggaged for darkness—
Oh, the straight train that into some sunlight
Not of our seeing ponders to plunge.

Oh, the slow hissing there, and the sleek
Watches held for decision. Hands
Waving at last. Deliberate rumble
Of leaving, leaving. Hunger for sun.

Yes, yes, off to the lighted
War that we so unsuccessfully see.
The only darkness that lasts is this one,
Up the iron slope, and all the way home.

You have not taken us now where the ground-flares
Flap to enclose you, stepping again
Out of our failure—we and the others—
All so sightless. Oh, the strange sun.

He's Coming

He's coming. He just called. Said he was coming,
Maybe, right away. O southern river,
Kiss that trestle sweetly,
Rub that upright gently,
And keep no train from home.

He's coming. Said all papers would be signed
By Sunday. O you honeysuckle timber,
Wrap those tulips, redbuds,
Hold those oaks from falling
Down on the right of way.

He's coming. Said expect him. There! what music
Rails already make, and pounded switches:
Wheels inside the south wind.
Where? O you the south wind,
Keep soft and strong today.

Save Us

Why, there he is now, as if the good gods
Had let him not die. But his look is the same—
O save us—as on the last day he was here,
And absently watched. He was no more then
Than one of us, watching; he hadn't been yet
The stumbled, the struck one; whom now the good gods
Deny us, sending the last that we saw.
He is no more here than one of us, watching;
And leaving, as if the whole thing were to happen
Again and again: the voyage, the guns—
O save us, for now we are big with foreknowledge.
This is the least of him. And he is leaving
Without the right word—with no word at all
To remember. What did we say? What now,
What now shall we say, as there the sharp shoulders
Wait for the moment that we shall do nothing—
Nothing, O save us, again and again.

The Great Wrath

It was cold, it was slow anger,
Gathered against the grain;
It was the consenting of soft valleys,
After all, to be volcano land.
It was the difficult decision,
Sailing, to murder murder.

And this was done. Historian,
Remember the fair time before.
Set down the peacefulness of that plantation.
Law was the bravest word among those towns
Whence, bitterly, brute wings
Took off to strangle strength.

It was a cold, a slow music,
Played with a grim skill,
Remote, in dragon places.
And it beat on to silence; rested only
When the raw noise it reared itself against
Was gone with the slayer, slain.

The Great Return

Someday ten million Ithacas will have them;
They will come steaming home, come banking home
Past the big cloud the god of our suspense
Built high above sweet springs and shingled houses.
Someday, someday, the oceans and the air,
Man-loud, will bear them hither in slow swarms—
Slow, but a host will gather, and long shores
Live with familiar feet, and inland acres
Shudder beneath fond weight, and cars and cattle
Caper again; the factories, the highways,
Fields, and old hedges musical with rain crows,
Parlors, and potato-scented kitchens,
Be as ten million nests for homing men.
Who as they nod and settle will remember
Others that never flew—the jungle holds them,
And the exploded abbey, the shrill street
Where snipers are no more; nor comrades either.
Sweet is the land that death too once desired,
Sweet the acknowledged waters, the roof ridges
That faded in a far dream or did not—
Not now, except for these who are the world's
Forever as they halfway too come home.

After the Great Victory

After the great victory a lonesome man
Unwounded went listening for what had stopped.
Not the guns merely, or spent fragmentation
Pattering on helmets: enough for a headache;
Remembering, he rubbed it. Not merely
Mired rations, and men with grey mouths
Thirstily swearing, not officers in first fear
Whispering impossible orders; the colonel
Shot half away and crying—old crow he was,
Cawing in blood on the ground, old black
Magnificent crow, tuning Italian forests.
Not Fortresses, riveting more sky,
Not mortars in the ravine, nor the calamitous
Heavies, rip and boom of a last judgment.
These, yes, but he could hear them if he tried.
The other—was it living? Did it ever
Live? The seventh sense he had then
Was full of it, he knew. But nowhere now.
Or did he listen wisely? Was the world
Hiding its heart? He listened, lonesome warrior,
And went crippled; not from fire but from no fire,
No echo out of the seventh cavern, cold
And inward evermore, a single secret
Dead with the colonel, crying—old crow
That shared it with him then, as danger shook
Both faces; but the shot one looked away,
And his last curse was music in the wood.

Nowhere, Nowhither

More than the remaining distance
Daunted him. That took but legs,
But counting druggedly the towns and miles,
And the slow tiles
That drained this dreary country into ditches
Where muskrats paddled. He, homecomer here,
Equally was searching the soft bank—
But time, not water; and he shrank
From the bleared vision
Of all their memories run so together,
With name and face now every color,
That the tired man who spoke
Would be but smoke,
But haze out of a history. Himself
Saw that way too from weariness: no wife
In the first warmth, no children clear of limb
Waiting in one place for him.
Nowhere, nowhither. But he straggled on,
Remembering old tales of brave return
And hoping some were true; and walking faster
As one suddenly seemed so—of the grown son
And the greyhound who ran to meet their master,
And the sweet mistress of the lighted hall
So still beyond; but loud in stall
His horses neighing,
And high in wind above it all,
Elms swaying.

And Premonition's Self

And premonition's self became afraid.
What men might do, might not do, what the storm,
The standstill, what the creeping waste of change—
Once messenger to those, but in its own mind
Gay, it now was gone about the eyes,
It staggered. There was nothing left to carry
But its first bulk, that went now with the time,
Breathing. It was one with us in doubt
Of darkness's near edge, of what would show
On future's face when miles had ticked away—
Then here it was, the monster. Here was what?
But premonition's self, in growing silent,
Had ceased except as one of us who waited,
Except as one more life that listened, breathing.

HOT HEAVEN

Hot Heaven

Cool night, cool night out of Canada,
Scatter bright fires over Cornwall.
There! Vega through the frosty trees
Burns all the hotter, and the Northern Cross
Flames in the Milky Way as ice flames,
Streaming with smoke of snow. Aquila
Tempers its wedge; and Corona,
Queen of horizon, kindles her last caverns.
Sagittarius is more on fire
For the cold waves he shoots through, for the chilblains
Bluing his fingers. Scorpio, late sunk,
Leaves, nevertheless, its double
Barb blazing. Fiercely, fiercely
Over Cornwall, cool night out of Canada,
Scatter these intensest embers.
Glitter with them. Let all hectic,
Hectic have hot heaven,
Frosty night.

The News of Snow

The news of snow full driven at the face,
Or settling, settling, not to be denied,
Comes on and on, as if the world had waited
Only till now to show its other side:
Then all at once, for whispers in the air
Say walls have turned and white is everywhere.

And it comes on. For not the cold, the blowing,
Not the shy rustle where the leaves were shed,
But always, always the arrival hither
Of what was yonder once, of what was dead:
This is the outer, this the ancient thing
That shrugs and comes, as if a shroud could sing.

As if the ash were all, the hoary cloak
Worlds wear to show that time is done with them;
As if immensity, that murdered earth,
Now cast its mold, its powdery diadem;
So the lost atoms, ending themselves here,
Whisper in white at so much nothing near.

False Summer

In the dead middle of the longest winter
There was an hour like this one, hot and still.
I can remember coming home by footpaths
Whitened as these, but not with daisy frill.

I can remember how the sun hung suddenly
Idle as I entered by the gate;
And flies from nowhere buzzed; and steadily, steadily
The eave troughs dripped, as if disconsolate.

But not so; that false summer was accepted
With the same happiness this true one hears.
Warmth rose, and water fell, and small musicians
Tumbled among the ghosts of the grass's spears.

If it was brief, so is the longest hay month,
When the sun dozes, dreaming that change is lost.
Time finds it with his terrible thin fingers,
That dice all day with honey and hoarfrost.

Coming Home Carelessly

Coming home carelessly,
Nine thoughts away,
The tenth took it in—So!
The dog days are over.

Sultriness never
Survived such a green
Last evening as lay,
Mint strip on the hills,

And sliced the long summer,
And sheared the heat's end.
But I came alone; so
Eleven is yours.

Looking Yonder

Ice on a hundred highways
Keeps seven cities home;
Yet keeps some there at windows,
Prisoners of room;

Keeps me, as morning glitters,
And the street steams with breath,
As blind to what is round me
As though this were death.

But it is looking yonder,
And what lives thus is warm
With something more than crystals
Comforting its form.

One small slope of mountain
May know when I come over
By how I name the meadows,
The moss ones, the clover;

By how I see through whiteness
To the least rock and mouse
Where ledge runs into woodland,
Opposite that house,

That house with sleepy buildings
Haloing its head;

I count the folded ladders,
The wood in its cold bed,

The kerosene, the hanging
Saws; and even by day
The stall with its hot lantern,
Lengthening wild hay.

The Mountain

The mountain he is more than there,
Than lying there northeasterly;
Than being where he is at all,
Eating horizon hungrily.

The mountain he is quieter
Than quickest glances tell to us;
A sudden look is what he likes,
Yet there he sleeps, mysterious.

The mountain runs a faster race,
From plain to plain, from slope to slope,
Than waves of sea, or over grass,
Rippling in wind, the antelope.

The mountain can be live, be dead;
His weight absents itself, returns;
The mountain he is masterly;
Concerns in him are unconcerns.

Camp Night

A little water will put out the fire.
But wait. A little wood will keep it breathing.
It is a heart we started with ten sticks
That now are nothing, like a hundred others
Shrunk to this hectic person whose last life
Would drain the whole cool forest if it could.
Another handful, then, though it is late.
So much in little, such a hungry principle:
We are not lightly to extinguish that.
Quiet a little longer, while it hisses
And settles, keeping secret the sore word
That soon enough its embers will forget.
Our own existence, partly. A wild piece
Of me and you we presently must drown.

Having Won

Dawn comes difficultly;
Strains, disinherited blood,
To ooze back through all distance;
Forces tough tissues, till with tiredness
Slowly they thin;
But sullenly, as if the red might fail:
Defeated morning, while one sleepy bird
Knows only that it sounded; a slim note
Kindling no others; and it grips again
The twig, night's tendon, tautening the deep.
But then companions brighten. Far and near,
Minute first flakes are shed, first glimpses spring
Of the new body, paling into strength
As now whole clusters fly,
Whirling and filling newborn everywhere
Translucently with music. The mad red
Grows milder, having won, and with this chorus
Whitens to silence. The full day has come,
The visionless, the deepless, to be seen through by all eyes
Of objects, and all animals and men.

The Chickadee

The chickadee has three short songs
To love the world with, spring and fall;
And winter,
For he loves it all.

And two of them are cherry sweet,
But one is diligent persimmon;
Children
Love the last, and women.

And it is cheerful at the door,
In snow, when nothing else will sing.
But woodsmen
Hear a different thing.

In ragged pines, in melting March,
Or in September's softer prime,
Two sounds,
Or three, in saddest time:

Most plaintive, as the happy heart
Can be, pretending. So they say,
Those men
Alone, and look away.

The Sparrow

Is there no All,
The sparrow in his small
Domed head asked darkly of himself?

Is there no One,
The sparrow in his dun
Wing coat said, hopping up the bush?

I have heard it—No—
But who in all this woe
Of winter watches each of us that flies?

Someone stands
And claps great hands
And smiles upon our smartness—someone does,

Or why such pride
In certain that have died,
As if a witness went with them to ground?

Is there no Him?
Why then these trim,
True bodies, all asunder, all the same?

There is—for see me now,
The sparrow said, and flew
Straight down, and flicked a grit of yellow up.

A Hundred Minnows

A hundred minnows, little-finger length,
Own the slim pond. In sets they make
Maneuver: all one way
Change-minded, yet of one mind where clear water
Clouds with their speed an instant;
All one speed, one purpose, as they veer
And suddenly close-circle; and some leap—
There! at an unseen fly,
There! at nothing at all.
Brown minnows, darkening daily
Since the thin time, the spring,
Since nothingness gave birth to such small bones,
Beat the soft water, fill
The wet world; as one,
Occupy movement, owning all August,
Proud minnows.

Tall Jack

The big bay stands in the rain with his blinders
Spattering drops and making him blink.
Tall Jack waits in the field for someone's
Step on the grass—not mine, I think.

The rain is only beginning, and so
He will be there still when I come and stand;
He will be indifferent and warm
Under the mane where I run my hand;

He will lower his great long head a little,
He will peer from his blinders round at me;
But not for this has he drooped in patience
With rainstreams darkening down each knee.

Not for this one who comes friendly,
And yet is alien as he strokes
Nose, flank, and shoulder—not for him
The rump in the cold rain steadily smokes,

Shifting its shape as the grey hind hooves
In turn lift upward, looking for dry.
Big Jack waits, and the hitch rope drips,
Drips, that the right one must untie.

Those Wings

"Giddup, giddup, you old forgotten
Hobbledyhorse, you goggle-eye!"
But the plowboy never saw that field
Where the young ravens used to fly.

"What's in your rotten bones today
That makes you clump and stumble so?"
The shadows of those morning wings
Beside these feet went poor and slow,

These foal's feet with their mother's racing
Down to the wood's edge where the spring
Bubbled forever—but "Giddup,
Giddup!" is all a boy can sing

Who never was told of the curly neck
And the tossed head that teased the mare;
Or the black shadows of the black
Evening wings outdistanced there;

Or the quaint mind that dew could feed
Between sweet intervals of grass;
Thinking then and thinking now:
Days of summer never pass.

Under Cover

Put it away in that building; rust and dust
And rats are there, and spiders, and dry rot;
But the roof is good, and so those two great robbers,
Rain and sun, will go and hunt elsewhere;
And so gravedigger time—old naked time
That moves without a shadow—he'll creep on
To things no hand has hidden. Lay it away,
For that is what men do. Time, sun, and rain
Would have all earth as one—look how they soak
And wither, and sink hugest objects in.
Even dark buildings; but forget, forget.
Think only of the open, and how smooth
Time keeps it with his tools of wet and dry.
Even stout rooftrees; but repair them now.
The difference between late death and soon
Is inches, time will mumble; yet men know
How golden is that space, how not to be spared.

Moonrise Limited

The low, the large, the umber moon
That suddenly we saw was sailing,
Sailing level with the train,
Sailing leftward and unlawful,
East as we were, east to ocean;
And its tender side cut steeples,
And it sliced at trees and cables
As it raced—a rearward madness,
Renegade to west and over,
Runaway from arch's calm.
Low and dizzy it went with us,
Out of the window south ahead;
And its soft flank was flattened, pressing
Spaces where it once had slept;
Pressing with us till we shuddered,
Laughing, and pulled down the shade.

It Was and It Was

It was and it was; that day, that day,
Born double, was time's twin-headed calf,
A monster if we ever saw one—yet
The four sweet eyes made all of us laugh.

Yet two of them had their terrible brown,
Dusk in the middle of innocent blue;
Their terrible black, for it was no color
At all our deep hilarity knew.

Under each face that squinted in wind
And reddened in so exciting a sun,
Behind each forehead the gravest delight
Lived for a day, and only that one.

Never again have I at least
And never I think have they, have they,
Smiled to the center: serious gods
Watching the whole world darken away.

Waterfall hours, with a hidden roar.
Noise at the heart that broke and broke.
Never again I think will eternity
Make and murder at one stroke.

The Little Cities

The little cities of New Orleans
Where the dead lie—
Tilted, flowering tombs inside four walls
Quiet and high—

The little streets, the temples in low rows
Where sisters sleep,
Where fathers of old families, old bones,
Old letters, weep:

No sweeter wind blows anywhere today
Than through these tufted
Crannies in the crumbled brick, these shelves
By slow truth shifted.

For here the rumor of ten thousand deaths
Is gentle, is soft;
Is January smiling; though all woe
Winters aloft.

GODS AWHILE

The burning cheeks of lovers, the stopped breath—
But then it comes again, and whispers death
So sweetly they will have no other hour
Than this their secret one—the mortal power
Of lovers is to waste all alien time
And wither every sound except this rhyme
Inside them, of the blood that doubly beats
And deafly; until even that retreats:
The last sense gone, as there they lie
Untouchable, and in their blisses die.

There is no death like this one of well lovers,
No woe like this that wonderfully hovers
Over good warmth and guesses when to fall,
Blanketing like night the world and all.
Like night, but it is day. No death, no woe
Save as they live again and call it so:
Again close clinging, and despising time
That does not strike with them, that does not climb
And break its waves forever on the shore
Of two in one, immortal here once more.

Unless

With lovers there is language
For everything but this:
The creeping cat of a desire
That springs, and will not miss
Unless the other one awhile
Too weary is—unless.

Neither lover learns, alas,
Unwritten, the cool sign:
No jungle now, no stealthy
Sweet fur, and whine
Of longing; only peace,
Peace be mine and thine.

So when by grace appearing
The leopards leap as one,
Each finds the other stranger
For what in dark is done;
Yet dreams then of no other world,
Secretless, like sun.

Down from the Waist They Are Centaurs

The cool fall, a little out
Then flowing down; the clean curve—
It might be woodland water, but it is
Dry fire: the burning secret of all men,
The precious danger seen and yet not seen,
Confessed when unconfessed.

Women do not know the might
They move in, cannot stand apart,
Stricken, and behold this sudden thing:
The wilderness they wade become aloud,
Alive; the ancient animal they drag
Breathing its full power.

Yet slyly, for the eyes of men,
Blasted, give their tongues a blindness,
Maddened, seem to close. The instantaneous
Look is all there is: bonfire of fancy,
Dampened in a moment by forgetting;
Or else—and then the blaze.

Relapse

The atoms of an old jealousy, rejoicing,
Gathered in him again. Oh, but they fell
Far upward to refind him. Once he had watched,
Once he had wondered proudly at his power
As down he seemed to shed them like shook sand:
Grit that had left him, master. Long, long ways
They plunged, they disappeared; and he was well
With smoothness, and his charity could smile.
He thought strength had done it. Then they poured,
Oh, upward; the deep void had topmost doors
That opened as the fall became a fountain.
Strength, but it was not his; nor ever had been;
The clear time between was hollow lie.
He heard them here, rejoicing in reunion:
Shape again, and function; a whole heart
To forage in; he felt them at their feeding.
So grace in him drained drearily away:
The freedom, the self-love, that now as sand
Thirsted in space's desert, the down gulf
Whence atoms had ascended. And still came.

Who Finds His Love

Who finds his love a whore at heart
Was mad to find it—why go there?
Why look? Why feel? For from the start
It must have been so everywhere.

It must have been that she would turn
When she did turn. But when was that?
Who played the ape? He will not learn;
There is no name for him or it.

There is no history of whore.
It heaves out of another time.
It is another horror—more
Than wildest madness will redeem.

For he is lost that now has looked,
And looking, found; and finding, felt.
Eternity's evil is unhooked
From the white wall, and slips its hilt,

And plunges through so thin and far
He cannot say what let the blood.
The horror now is not the scar,
But how this stillness shakes his bed.

The Bitterest Things

The bitterest things are sweets misunderstood,
Or worse, refused in fury: the struck face
Of Desdemona, doubted; the searched word
More innocent than milk, but by this madness
Curdled; such a forearm as Diana
Shed once like a shadow over pain,
Chopped into lecher's meat, the eye despising
What is most whole, most his, the heart distributing
Minced gifts to others; jealous generosity
Letting the benefactor's own best blood.
The bitterest is the purest; but mistaken,
Most poisonous. To her, and then to him.
For he is last to know what lavish gold
He vinagered, what water, brackish now,
Is spiderless no more; and that he drinks it.

Consider, Man

Guilty lover of that queen,
That spider lady whose torn web
Spangles with such pretty tears,
Consider, man, the cost to her
Whose luxury is suffering.

Consider if you had not come
And strung with her those dusky strands
In the dark corner where confusion weeps:
Consider, man, the cost to one
Whose whole sweet wealth is suffering.

She will not say so, guilty drone
Who helped her weave the pattern out;
She charges you with ruin done;
But every rent is riches there;
Consider, man, the suffering.

Consider well the dreary cost
Of not a sigh in all that silk;
In all that dancing no sweet death;
Her majesty considers, man,
What she must owe you, suffering.

Recovery

The lump of sore silence
In two throats at once
(The slenderer, sweet-filling,
Outsuffered its mate),

The lump, the unspeakable,
Lay for too long
Not to go slowly;
But then it was gone;

And now it seemed sudden,
As if the world sang
Six hundred sunrises
Together in ring;

Together like minutes,
Slumbrous in time,
Till gong! till the chorus,
Awful in cry,

Of stars understanding
The multiple dark:
Joy in two persons,
Secret, at work.

Sleep, Sleep

Sleep, sleep, slug in the sun,
Be limp forever, like warm grass.
Be lost to shape, be legs and arms,
Be body separate, be sweet soul
That melts and spreads like innocent spring
When time undoes it. Be green song
That sighs unto itself and dozes;
Dries, and into summer brown
Relaxes. So be young and dead,
Beloved, be as nothing there,
There in the sun while I keep watch,
There with the grass while I remember.
Sleep, sleep, beloved of worlds
That will be jealous, will awake you.
Sleep, until they stand and ask
Who this was by you all the while.
Forget me now, though, sleep and sleep,
Slug of my heart, O nothing of mine.

The Mistress

Nothing, no one comes to see
Honorable him and me.

Has either of us turned to snow?
Gossip ended long ago.

Was I cheap for him or dear?
Nothing, nothing passes here.

But one of us did not mistake.
I lie and say it, wide awake;

And do not think his doubt has come
Even to that simple sum.

It is not backward that he counts
The happiness my lips pronounce.

Having never to decide
Is how he loves me still, his bride.

WORDS FOR MUSIC MORE OR LESS

Then Both Shall Be

When icicles around the earth
Are played upon by one long wind,
And crickets winter in warm grass,
Then I shall be as once I was.

When midnight mushrooms march away
And owls are motherly to mice,
And there is only one great star,
Then you will be as once you were.

When rocks remember being fire
And time to come ticks on the wall,
And truth is mirror of each man,
Then both shall be as both have been.

And Not My Wounds

Tell him I was beautiful,
Tell him I walked well;
Tell him I was columbine,
Brown daisy, and harebell.

He talked of these things that I was,
And called the world to see,
Like one who had created them,
Then manufactured me.

Tell him I am stars by night,
And stillness by noonday.
For he must know, that left me here,
Nothing has gone away;

Nothing is dead or different—
Tell him, and make sure.
For he must understand that I
And not my wounds endure.

Will He Come Back?

Will he come back, O will he, will he,
Dandelion and yellow daisy?
    He will come back to you, tall daughter,
    When loving him is easy.

Will he come back to me, O will he,
Horses, horses, wild in the meadow?
    He will come back with ice in August,
    And sunshine in shadow.

Will he come back, O will he, will he,
Minnows, minnows, deep in the pond?
    He will come back when air is water,
    And the high sky is sand.

Will he come back to me, O will he,
Midnight moth on the windowpane?
    He will come back when I, when I do—
    Whisk! and I try again.

Will he come back, O will he, will he,
Heart in my body, weakly crying?
    He will come back when you can no longer
    Hear what I am saying.

Soft, Soft, Soft

Soft, soft, soft
Is her gazing when I leave her and am gone;
When I leave her;
Soft is her coming, coming where I am,
By sunlight or by moonlight, halfway around the world.

Soft is my truelove's
Looking when she listens, listens to my name;
Just listens;
Soft is how she ever is, coming, staying,
By sleepy night, by sleepy noon, my fair love.

Strong, strong, strong
Is her softness that will never, never change;
Never change;
As water to be water, as air being air,
Firm, firm, firm is the purpose of my love.

But never, never hard
Is the looking of my love, lonesome love,
When I come;
Soft is the waiting, the waiting of her eyes
Halfway around the water world and sweet dry land.

One Red Rose

My love she is a rose that lives
When nothing else does any longer.
Winter deepens and worlds die,
But one red rose meanwhile is stronger.

My love is that one, and I live
Because she does, in wind and rain
That are as warm as when we first
Were slips of summer to be slain.

Yet this my rose, outliving frost,
Is fresher now than any new one.
She alone, of all that smile,
Is red and loving, is the true one.

Where She Is Now

Be quiet, and the words will slide
In slowly, and their laziness
Best tell how you, best lover,
Love her without sound at all.
You do, so why look then for words?
Tell who? the wind? Well, you the wind,
Take this and lose it for him somewhere,
Lazy lover who would sing.

Where she is now, with people,
Do passages and rooms,
Do table edges know it,
The sweetness of her clothes?

Does wood she touches tremble
That such a person moves,
Remembering me always?
For this she sweetly does;

And swings me with her, modest,
A thought upon her thighs,
A lover there, and lazy,
Till both of us come home.

Then who but I, unwrapping,
Will know it all the night:
This looseness to the center,
And sweetness every part?

Sometimes I Believe

She loves me or she loves me not,
I am a fool, a wise man.
Sometimes I believe I know;
Then she is wild, is woman.

Some days she is worldly kind,
As to the millionth beggar.
I think it is for me she feels,
Then find I was but neighbor.

Some days when I least am looking
Love comes to my shoulder.
Sits and sings; but she has sent
Nothing, she says, from her.

There she lies, in sleepy shade,
And all her blood, I fancy,
Blesses the sharp thought of one
Who like a thief will enter.

So shall I slip and with outrage
Be winner of that warmness?
Sometimes I believe I see
She loves no one, this woman.

Burden of Ornament

My darling with the single daisy,
Porcelain, pinned in her hair,
On other afternoons will glitter
With earrings, silver, or a fair
Gold brooch; that supper changes
Into an apron, crimson, there.

My darling in these dolorous days
Does all the work of courting birds;
Or in far places, long ago,
Of Scythian men, who to be lords
Went forth in feathers; or of gods
Whom still a band of glory girds.

My darling with sweet-william nosegay,
Artful, under slope of breast,
Or giant buckle, set loquacious
Over that littleness, her waist,
My darling bears the ancient burden
Smiling; nor doth dream of rest.

The Bridegroom's Chantey

When I was farther away than a ship
Would show—two beautiful eyes in a tower—
The wind here was the same dry wind
That kissed my sails a certain hour.

When I was longer away than a clock,
Remembering, could tell in the room,
Those birds there, with their beautiful backs,
Were the same three that sat on my boom.

When I came lonely into port,
The hill of ocean all behind,
What made my pillow that night so soft
Except these beautiful stars that shined?

When I am again with you, with you—
Beautiful lips that open so free—
Why do you think you must deny
You sent the whole world after me?

Song of the Two Vagrants

Alone I came to cool Manhattan,
On a fine day in friendless fall;
And would have left it but for someone,
Someone I don't blame at all.

Neither for goodness that I stayed with—
Oh, the short time when nights were long—
Nor the quick change in her that banished,
Banished me: it was not wrong.

Yet who so lonely on the road now?
Again I wander, and years die;
And maybe where she lives is marble,
And someone's luck it is to lie—

Oh, that's the reason time goes slowly,
Wandering with me far to west;
Remembering those sweet long evenings,
And the low voice that gave us rest;

And the gold hair that once in hallways
Burned in the darkness, being kissed.
Oh, time and I have turned from many,
But she was the one, the one we missed.

Unto Death

He made her love him, oh, he did,
He did, and it was unto death;
Except that government of sighs
Imperfect is, and of this breath
We do not notice, in or out,
So wantonly it wandereth.

Into her sleep and out again:
Perhaps it was the wayward night;
Perhaps it was the deed of stars
Whereunder light became her light.
Or what if some lean wanderer
Had looked too long at her and bright?

She would not say, nor could he ask,
So faithfully she tended him.
She did, and it was unto death;
Except for certain sudden dim
Midsummer dusks when a ghost walked
Between them, luminous and slim.

Dunce's Song

The wind that comes, the wind that goes,
Never tells me what it knows.
The wind is witness of all things—
Of water's birth, of Saturn's rings,
Of sin's undoing, of love's laws,
And revolutions without cause—
But still my face is famine lean;
The wind that sees cannot be seen.
If I could turn a sudden head,
Sidewise perhaps, as the wind sped
And its dark edges rippled by,
I might grow wise enough to die.
But here I stand and only know:
Wind come, wind go.

Beggar's Beatitude

In wanderment I came to where—
In ragged woe did I arrive—
Suddenly I stumbled, for
The corners of the world were five.

Direction lost its way among
Wild grasses where the pavement stopped.
And I fell down as in a web,
A flowery web whence sparrows hopped

And sang that in my laziment
I had come home to stars at last;
For that was how this pasture spread,
Soft as midnight, and more vast.

Direction was no tyrant there;
The sparrows, though in darkness, sang;
Yet morning moved among the stars,
And glory in me rang and rang

As round and round the world's five corners
Spun—and yet no sound was made—
As if all light took me for cause,
In spanglement forever laid.

Bay-Window Ballad

The old man in the window,
With his hair all combed,
The old man in the window
Will drive no more.

He watches down the valley,
In his collar and clean cuffs,
He watches down the valley
As the teams come up.

There, by the big rock,
Seventy Junes ago,
There, by the big rock,
He tipped his load.

How the old one scolded,
The old one who is gone;
But that old, old one
Never was young;

Never at this window,
With his face all washed,
Never at this window
Tapped the glass.

Tap! and the great roans
Answer with their feet;
Tap! and a grandson
Whirls his hat.

What's Wrong?

Said the engineer to the fireman,
"What's happened? He didn't come out."
Said the fireman, pulling the bell cord,
"That's for old Jiminy Trout.

"Didn't you hear? His daughter—
Beautiful, some say—
Found him dead as a cricket
On the doorstone yesterday.

"Found him after we passed here—
Remember how he waved?
As always; but it took him
Most of the strength he had saved.

"The rest of it he sat down with,
And saw us around the curve.
That's for you, old Jiminy,
But it isn't what you deserve.

"It ought to be slow and heavy,
A toller, and doleful long."
The engineer leaned over:
"What did you say? What's wrong?"

Until, Until

How much the place pleased him
He never would tell,
Any more than the clapper,
Deserting the bell,
Will swing to no purpose
In vacancy's well.

They played on each other,
He and that ground;
It was not for a stranger
He struck the icebound,
The butterfly meadows
To alternate sound.

It was not for immensity's
Ear that he sang
As deep the lane listened
And rough the wood rang;
Then silence, as sometimes
The whole bronze will hang,

And the swinger within it,
Sleepily still,
Is strong to no purpose,
Is iron without will,
Until the wind wakens—
Until, until.

The Wind Has Changed

South wind, suddenly
Cool among the curtains,
Cunning as the dark is
To pour indoors;

South wind, thrusting,
Thrusting into corners,
Without any keenness
Your sweet force comes.

South wind, gentlest
Of night's old changes,
South wind, softest
For all your power,

South wind, south wind,
Loosen every heart here,
Sweeten every forehead,
With memory of rain.

The Sad Child's Song

Heavy, Heavy, hangs in my head.
Not over, over, not superfine.
In here, in my head, hangs Heavy, Heavy,
And nobody knows.
Dead down he hangs,
Nor sweats, nor swings;
Pure weight, pure lump, is Heavy in here,
Here in my head where nobody sees.
Not over, over, not lucky and fine,
Not something for others, laughing, to say
Is mine if I want it, mine, is mine.
What shall the owner do to redeem it?
I can do nothing with Heavy in here,
Here in my head; and nobody helps.
Dead weight he hangs,
Pure lump, nor swings.
Heavy, Heavy, is all I have.
Heavy, oh Heavy, is mine to keep.

The Glad Child's Song

Where are we now,
Says thistle ball,
And so say I, and so say I.

Me and my body
Went off together,
But who cares where, but who cares where?

Nobody guesses
That here we are yet,
With people around, with people around.

What do they notice,
My body or me?
And which of us cares, and which of us cares?

One of us changed,
Yes, but he did,
Into a dancer, into a dancer,

And whirls the other one,
Oh, so lightly,
Oh, so lightly, oh, so lightly,

Around and around,
And neither will ever,
And neither will ever
Be tired any more, be tired any more.

How Shall We Know Them?

How shall we know him,
The man he will be?
Not by this walking
So far and lonely.

How shall we know her
When ladytime comes?
Not by this husky
Song that she hums.

Both are outlasting
Already this dim,
This pretty believing
That she is of him,

That he is of her,
For the two are but one.
How shall we know them
When April is done?

Summer and winter,
The dry and the cold—
How shall we know them
When they are old?

We shall not know them,
Having been wrong.

True love walks in him
Lonely and long.

We shall not know them,
Having this doubt.
True love forever
Sleeps in her throat.

Chipmunk, Chipmunk

Chipmunk, chipmunk, little and small,
Roll your stripes into a ball.

White horse, white horse, winter is warm
With a shaggy coat for wind and storm.

Owl, owl in the hemlock tree,
Hoot till morning for all of me.

Robber, robber, snug in your den,
Pick the bones of our old hen.

Lighthouse, lighthouse, tall by the shore,
Shine on the shipwreck no more.

Maple, maple over this roof,
What do you listen to, far off?

Train, train around Great Hill,
Whistle again and then be still.

Down Dip the Branches

Down dip the branches,
The long leafy branches,
Down dip the branches
To bring old robin in.

Underneath the haytops,
The warm windy haytops,
Underneath the haytops
The mice are creeping home.

Soon it will be sunset,
Red and yellow sunset,
Soon it will be sunset,
With everything indoors.

Apples for supper.
Sing, sing for supper.
After, after supper,
Sing awhile in bed.

Mouse in the meadow,
The green sleepy meadow,
Mouse in the meadow,
Fold your little paws.

Robin in the branches,
The dark sleepy branches,
Old robin in the branches,
Shut, shut, shut your eyes.

Where Did He Run to?

Where did he run to,
That old rooster?
Fox, fox,
How fast did he run?

Where is the mule gone,
That old rope-tail?
Manger, manger,
Where is the mule?

Where are the kittens
The old black cat had?
Blinker, Blinker,
Where are the kittens?

Where does the dog sleep,
That old shepherd?
Lambs on the mountain,
Where is your dog?

Where is the big boy
That swung on the gatepost?
Bedclothes, bedclothes,
Where is the boy?

Old Ben Golliday

Old Ben Golliday
Jumped off the wagon box,
And trotted with his horses,
Clop, clop, clop.

Old Ben Golliday
Was angry with his little wife,
And didn't see her bonnet strings
Fly, fly, fly.

Didn't look around
At the thank-you-mam, thank-you-mam,
Didn't see her somersault
High, high, high.

Old Ben Golliday
Trotted to the barn door,
And went in with his horses
To sleep, sleep, sleep.

Old Ben Golliday,
Dozing in the manger there,
Don't you know your little wife
Sits in the sky?

Old Ben Golliday,
Who will get your dinner now,
Who will sew your buttons on?
My, my, my!

Sleep, Grandmother

Sleep, grandmother, sleep.
The rocking chair is ready to go,
And harness bells are hung in a row
As once you heard them
In soft snow.

Sleep, grandmother, sleep.
Your sons are little and silly again;
Your daughters are five and seven and ten;
And he that is gone
Was not gone then.

Sleep, grandmother, sleep.
The sleigh comes out of the winter woods
And carries you all in boots and hoods
To town for candy
And white dress goods.

Sleep, grandmother, sleep.
The rocking chair is old as the floor,
But there he nods, at the noisy door,
For you to be dancing
One dance more.

He Cut One Finger

He cut one finger
And the other finger bled.
He cut off his head;
But he didn't have another,
So he's dead.

He shut one eye
And the other eye was gone.
He put his glasses on;
But he couldn't see to see,
So he's done.

The dwarf ate the giant
To become a giant too.
He grew and he grew,
But he couldn't hold him all,
So he's through.

The cot became a bed
And the bed became a boat.
But the boat couldn't float,
Being heavy; and the lights
Went out.